Strawber

GW00870025

Victoria
Lynn

Illustrations
by Sarah Ditterline

For the People I Love Most

Contents...

the simple ...

tea & honey

hair tied up in a knot,
cup of tea in one hand,
toast drenched with honey
in the other
she sits cross legged on the mattress
her eyes widen
her pale lips open slightly
goosebumps rise on her bare legs
and when the door swings open
she's been waiting for his return

simply content

the sweater hangs loosely on her tiny frame
pale skin exposed from the waste down
snow settles onto the windowsill
a book dangles from her hand
steam evaporates from the tea
her hair lays awry
she sits cross-legged
kitten in her lap
book in hand
legs bare
tea cold

sunflowers kiss the sun

freckles splattered across her face
she dances to the drum of nature
the hum of the bees
the swaying of the trees
the gentle wind pushing her forward
bare feet sink into fresh dirt
arms above her head
she sings along with the birds
and the crickets
she follows their rhythm
through the sunflowers
through the tall grass
the meadows that go on endlessly

human

but what if
we were nothing
didn't exist at all
aliens to our own troubled souls

within the trees

flowers tangle in her hair
she runs through the trees
to follow the moon
soft dirt sinks beneath
every barefoot step
she doesn't watch where
she's going
stars guide her way
she embraces nature's gentle touch
as it nudges her forward
blindly and carelessly she hums
her heart knows this is it
this is where she belongs

i wish

sometimes i wished the sun
shone more than the moon

track 15

time suspends
i'm moving backwards
eyes wide
through a dark tunnel
vision blurs
my eyes close
all aboard
i'm tumbling forward
feet shuffle
heavy breath
is this seat taken?
music blares
but barely audible
guy next to me
nods along
i start to hum
my heart throbs
to the rhythm of the tracks

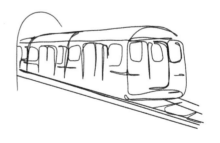

sunny feelings

like sunflowers we chase the sun
basking in its warmth

tiny moments

it's the simple things
the sun
the moon
your hand in mine

peaceful rest

her glasses rest
on the tip of her nose
and a book lays open
on her chest
it rises and falls
with each puff
of air that escapes
her parted lips

earth's story

she wonders about the world
about the people
that surround her
each one with a story
of their own
that forms and tangles
into other stories
each one creating just one
story of our existence
our entire life is just one story
that the world tells
and we are it

luna & sol

she lives for the moon
but dances with the sun

handcuffs

she freed herself
from the constraints
of the world
by turning to nature

impatient desire

sometimes but just sometimes
the sunflowers will turn to the moon
and forget the sun was there all along

wildflower

she had the wild kind of hair
reaching down the middle of her back
with waves and flowers
entwined in every twist

all mine

the sun and
the moon
are mine

moonlight

the moon summons me
i slip into the dark
sleep in the corners of my eyes
barefoot i walk across the gravel
till my feet sink into sand
i follow the path it creates
let the shadows slip behind
the ink black water
holds a sliver of light
the moon allowed to fall upon it
i dip my toe just under the surface
i take a deep breath and dive in

the unknown

the moon's reflection
was in her eyes
she dreamed of space
and the world beyond
she owned the stars
she claimed the night
when the milky way
made its appearance
she believes we're more
then what's here on earth
she dreamed of the people
we've never meet
the souls that are waiting for us
on the other side
what life could be
what life was
what in all pureness
it meant to be alive

the shadows

for some the dark is terrifying
but others thrive

come play with me

it's when the stars and the moon
come out to play
that i feel the most alive

phish

her hair lays wild
her black shorts frayed
a beer foams over the edge
threatens to tumble out
as each note of the song
sends her hips swaying
her bare feet
sink into the grass
he stands next to her
head nodding along
he's got his air guitar
out and jamming
they shout each note
knowing every word
they sing along to
a day that will turn into night
and a night they will never forget

not a cliche

like rainbows and butterflies
she makes earth smile

simple prayers

most people chase the sun
but here i am praying for the moon

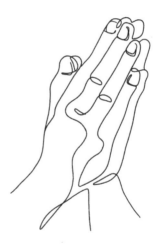

to be like you

huge steps with tiny feet trailing behind
she always looked up to you
aspired to be like you
she watched your every move
she mimicked every step
the way the lipstick covered her lips
the curls bounced to the middle of her back
she tried to read the books you read
tried to cook the way you did
her smile was yours
her laugh sounded the same
she could tell you anything
and you were her best friend
she dreamed to be a mother like you

strawberry wine

she was nothing but the sun and the moon,
as beautiful as a sunflower,
and as sweet as strawberry wine

the affection ...

daisies

she lays, head turned toward the sky
mind rested on earth's pillow
he notices the sun in her eyes
studies each freckle
that scatter across her nose
the rise and fall of her chest
the pale pink of her lips
he picks a daisy
brushes a curl away
and tucks it behind her ear

green tea

black chipped nails
a balcony faces the sea
cherry blossoms drift in the breeze
a page turns in the book on her lap
legs cross over one another
strands of her hair hover around her face
freckles dot her nose and cheeks
sun kisses the depths of her eyes
a Buddha statue in the corner
green tea at her feet
the boy admiring her from behind
moonlight shimmering off her exposed shoulder
smooth skin he wants to kiss
run the palms of his hands against
she lets out a laugh
he smiles to her back
she turns with a grin crinkling the corners of her eyes
he slips down behind her engulfs her into his arms
the book falls to the side
the ocean gently crashes to the shore
the moonlight shines in her eyes
he kisses her neck
and whispers *forever*

whiskey bottles

whiskey was on their breath
hair tangled in his hand
their bodies intertwined as one

to be little

she holds their pinkies
with tiny hands
looking up at
two people
she loves the most
and that love her more

always loving you

don't put me down
dance with me through the night
my little hand wrapped around your finger
my love wound tight around your heart
the twinkle in your eye
as we spin around the room
time twirling around us
i am two
before you knew it i was turning twenty-two
went from balloon animals
to makeup
but always loving you
forever your princess and grand daughter
although i may get older
and may outgrow your arms
you have to know
i'll never outgrow your heart
i am blessed to have you
to call my pops

sun kisses

a single sheet drapes her naked body
hair up in a messy knot
green eyes intensified by the light
she rolls over to face you
her teeth graze your ear
a smile threatens your sincerity
she throws her arms around you
you pull her in
lavender engulfs you
and you breath it in
head buried in her neck
you love her

eight months

moonlight wraps around her bare shoulders
hands resting gently on her pregnant belly
she stares out the window
the drapes create shadows as they sway
her husband lies silently in bed
with the white sheets pulled under his chin
fresh stubble forms a crescent
little puffs of breath flee from his mouth
she hums quietly to herself
a lullaby for the baby
about the moon and the sea
her face scrunches
freckles pinched together
as the baby tenderly kicks
her lips slightly part
eyes soften and she continues to hum

love me

you say you love me
and i believe you
not because of the words
but the kisses you plant
upon my forehead
my hand held in yours
the way you watch me
when i'm reading a good book
the way you kiss me at night
the way you hold me

with you

your eyes tell me
i am home

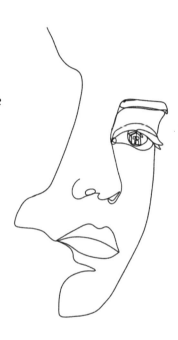

radiant eyes

her eyes shone brighter
then the sun for him

i say i do

flowers encircle her head
her glow captivates all
as she floats down the aisle
the train of her dress trails behind
her face says it all
tears threaten to spill out
and ruin her makeup
a smile of pure happiness
forms at the corners of her mouth
he has found his forever
as she has found hers
she takes his hand
he whispers *you are beautiful*
as they begin their journey together

her laugh

he sees her from the window
hears her laugh as her head tilts back
her shoulders rise and fall
a book held loosely in her hand
her nose scrunches
freckles pinch together
he finds himself smiling
he's laughing and he has no idea why
her laugh is contagious
he wants to be in this moment with her
he loves to see her happy
he loves that she is his

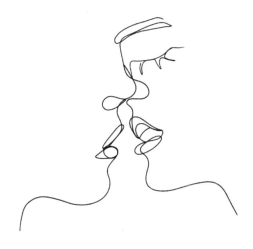

one kiss

he kissed me once
that's all it took
for me to be his

daddy's girl

she was her daddy's girl
like him she could not
get enough of the ocean

carefree

he held her hand
to guide her over puddles
but she jumped right in

your stare

your eyes see through me
as i melt at your feet

love like the wind

she was his whole world
the moon and the stars
the sun and the ocean
the long tall grass
and the taller sunflowers
the gentle breeze
that eased around him
just like her touch
her breath was sweet
with a hint of strawberries

i need you

her presence embodies you
it empowers you
it lights you from the dark depths
you realize you need her more then you
need water
or air
or anything else on this earth
she has become
all of the essentials
you don't know when it happened
but you know it did

you

you watch her every move
the way she laughs
from deep deep down
letting her shoulders rise up
scrunching her nose
while she covers her mouth
with her delicate hand
you trace her body with your mind
every curve every angle
from her toes
up to the crown of her head
you listen to the way she breathes
letting each small puff of breath
fill your ears
you watch as she sleeps
noticing the way her chest rises
then falls gently down
you mark each rise
as a beat in your head
as if you were composing a symphony
you pay attention when she talks
hanging on every word
as if you would fall off the edge of the world
if you didn't

love and thorns

love wound around our hearts
like two flowers grown together
building blindless love within
with thorns that could tear us apart
or protect us from the world's touch

backyard daisy

she's out in the garden
knees deep in dirt
her jean shorts
cut a little too high
her hair up in a knot
freckles crisscross
her cheeks
as a bead of sweat
forms on her brow
she swipes it away
with the back of her hand
leaving dirt streaked
right above her green eyes
she turns around
have you been there the whole time
i smile and sink down behind her
i whisper *yes* in her ear
goosebumps emerge
on her bare shoulders
i kiss them away

wrinkled kisses

she tends to live among the stars
letting her daydreams get the best of her
envisioning what her life will look like
what she will look like
what her future kids will look like
she dreams of getting old
and being so in love
giving each other wrinkled kisses
filled with love and laughter
she dreams of the perfect moments
and the milestones
their first home together
their first baby
the trips they'll go on
she's not naive she knows
there will be struggles
and curve balls sent their way
because that's what life is
but she knows they're stronger
and anyway, she can chose to
live among the stars anytime she wants
as long as he is by her side

safe house

it's nestled up beside him
that she felt most safe
with white sheets tucked under her chin
his strong arm wrapped around her
listened to the drum of his heart
as he breathed
feeling his chest rise and fall
with every silent puff of breath
he pulled her in closer
she felt the warmth of his skin
through her thin t-shirt
she felt at home

he hung the galaxy

sometimes it feels
like the moon the sun and the stars
are in hiding
leaving everything blank
making her feel empty inside
no light shining through
alone in mass emptiness
and then she hears his voice
faintly, very soft in the distance
calling to her
trying to bring her back into the light
with the moon the sun and the stars
her heart gives off a faint glow
with every word he whispers
it gets louder as she listens
and her heart glows brighter
without him she'd be left alone in the vast
emptiness of a galaxy with no moon no sun
and no stars

my king

he knelt on one knee
and she knew before this moment
that this moment would always come
she just didn't know when
she stood frozen in place
a tidal wave of emotion welled up inside her
but she did not falter
her heart thudded loud in her chest
with the crashing waves on the beach below
he took her hand
eyes shining bright with excitement and fear
he stared up at her
he asked a question
she let out a breath
she didn't realize she was holding

the ache...

broken

she sank to the bathroom floor
spine pressed against the tub
her hair lay awry encircling her face
oval eyes wide as they brimmed with tears
she placed her palms flat against her ears
as if to block out the noise
letters strung together forming words
she didn't want to hear

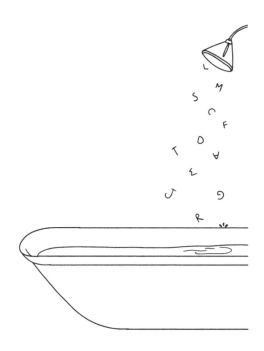

limbo

the world is upside down
or maybe it's right side up
but you're not
you're teetering on the edge
waiting for something to happen
spinning out of control
as the world moves on without you
falling into blank space

through space

her eyes used to show the galaxy
she was always up in the stars
twirling through the milky way
light radiating off of her
but a space vacuum forms
the stars burn out
the milky way disappears
she's left in a daze
hurtling towards earth
where her eyes remain vacant

falling to pieces

he sits hands shaking
tears fall from his eyes
as he stares down at the
old blue worn out carpet
millions of thoughts
race through his mind
only ones important
his brown hair is a wavy mess
upon his tired head
his nails are bitten to pieces
a nervous habit he just picked up
his jeans are faded and he forgot shoes
his toes rest on the hard green chair
the same green chair someone else sat in
just like him at a loss for words
he feels someone's hand on his shoulder
he slowly looks up to see it's the doctor
words are formed
it sounds muffled
his lips form a tight line
he runs a shaky hand through his hair
and runs it over his eyes and mouth
he slumps back into the chair defeated

vacant

she slams the door
his face was there
she clutches her chest
a glimpse of herself is noticed
gripping onto the sink she stares
her body lowers along the tub
he calls to her
he gently knocks on the door
she doesn't hear
all she hears is static
her body empty of emotion
raw and vulnerable
left covered in invisible scars
he slides down against the door
palm reaching out
helpless and hopeless
he calls to her
tears silently escaping their prison
but she's not there

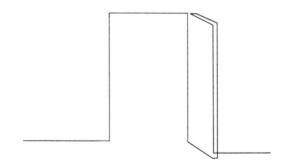

mentally where

sometimes i think
sometimes i don't
when i care
when i don't
i'm mentally here
i'm mentally there
my mind drifting
the blue seas
the rocky shores
your eyes
my lips
i'm here you're there

thoughts of her

he sails towards the dock
maneuvering the boat
beer in hand as he climbs up
he looks out into the endless
mix of sea and sky
his teeth glow against
the backdrop of the moon
he smiles combing his fingers
through his sea salt hair
he thinks *I miss her*
swears he can see
her moonlit shoulders
emerging from the water
her bright blue eyes
in the reflection
a single tear rebels
escaping his eye
and rolls down his
unshaven cheek
he blows a kiss to the sea
and turns and leaves

troubled

eyes clouded over
eyebrows knit together
jaw clenched tight
she was scared
she tried not to show it
hands formed in fists
she was ready to fight

home

she glances at an empty bed
sheets ruffled not made
from the night before
pillows tossed
she's restless when he's not there
she sighs and looks away
she wishes to herself
she wishes for the day
when he'll come home

the bed won't be empty
sheets will be tangled around them
pillows in their place
she'll be happy
she'll smile
she'll whisper *he's home*

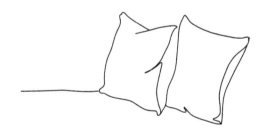

worthless

you say you're perfect
all i see are flaws
you always put me down
my worth is little
when it comes to you

it's over

your lips slur words you want to mean
behind each scotch influenced breath
you're rambling trying to fix the inevitable
the lights left their eyes

do you know?

death is just a word
left with so much unknown
we know death occurs
we know the meaning
but we don't really know

feeling frail

his voice was left weak
tired from the strain
of what became
everyday life

For Rob,
the love of my life
you are my moon and my stars
my sun and my ocean
my whole world

Acknowledgments...

I'd like to thank all my friends and family that have supported and motivated me throughout this experience. I want to give a special shout out to the following people:

Mom and Dad for making my dreams and goals become reality by enrolling me in Endicott College's English program.

Rob my fiancé and future husband for always motivating me, believing in me, and loving me. I couldn't have done it without your love and support, I love you so much!

My sister Julianna for sitting by my side bouncing ideas back and forth and keeping me motivated, focused, and excited.

My brother Alec for supporting me and always being my photographer and photo editor.

My great friend, Alex Munteanu, is endlessly listening and giving me constructive criticism on my poetry, short stories, and ideas. A special thank you for editing my first book!

My professors from Endicott have helped shape me into the writer I am today, thank you Professor Daniel Sklar and Samuel Alexander.

My wonderful and talented illustrator Sarah Ditterline for bringing my vision to life. You can follow her on Instagram @saarahgraphics

About the Author

Victoria Lynn is a writer from Long Island, New York. She received her Bachelor of Arts in English with a concentration in Creative Writing at Endicott College. Victoria has been published by both Z Publishing House and Ibbetson Street Press numerous times.

She finds inspiration through nature, especially through the ocean and the moon. You can find her sipping wine on a beach somewhere with a book in her hand.

Milton Keynes UK
Ingram Content Group UK Ltd.
UKHW051711091223
434089UK00017B/133

9 781034 409465